SandCastle™

Animal Homes

Home
Sweet
Cave

Mary Elizabeth Salzmann

CONSULTING EDITOR, DIANE CRAIG, M.A./READING SPECIALIST

A Division of ABDO
ABDO
Publishing Company

visit us at www.abdopublishing.com

Printed in the United States of America, North Mankato, Minnesota
062011
092011

 PRINTED ON RECYCLED PAPER

Editor: Katherine Hengel
Content Developer: Nancy Tuminelly
Cover and Interior Design and Production: Anders Hanson, Mighty Media, Inc.
Photo Credits: Shutterstock, Jernej Polajnar (pp. 16-17; image avilable for reuse under the Creative Commons license), Peter Arnold (S.J. Krasemann, Heuclin Daniel), iStockPhoto (Alexander Klemm)

Library of Congress Cataloging-in-Publication Data
Salzmann, Mary Elizabeth, 1968-
 Home sweet cave / Mary Elizabeth Salzmann.
    p. cm. -- (Animal homes)
 ISBN 978-1-61714-816-3
1. Cave animals--Juvenile literature. 2. Animals--Habitations--Juvenile literature. I. Title.
QL117.S25 2012
591.56´4--dc22
                    2010053040

SANDCASTLE™ LEVEL: TRANSITIONAL

SandCastle™ books are created by a team of professional educators, reading specialists, and content developers around five essential components—phonemic awareness, phonics, vocabulary, text comprehension, and fluency—to assist young readers as they develop reading skills and strategies and increase their general knowledge. All books are written, reviewed, and leveled for guided reading, early reading intervention, and Accelerated Reader® programs for use in shared, guided, and independent reading and writing activities to support a balanced approach to literacy instruction. The SandCastle™ series has four levels that correspond to early literacy development. The levels are provided to help teachers and parents select appropriate books for young readers.

Emerging Readers
(no flags)

Beginning Readers
(1 flag)

Transitional Readers
(2 flags)

Fluent Readers
(3 flags)

Contents

What Is a Cave?

A cave is an open space under the ground. Caves can be filled with air or water. Caves are very dark. Little or no sunlight shines into a cave.

Animals and Caves

Over time, animals change to make living in caves easier. Many cave animals can't see well, or at all. But their senses of hearing, touch, and **smell** are often very strong.

7

Vampire bats live in caves.

Vampire bats spend the day hanging upside down in caves. The vampire bat is the only **mammal** that just eats blood.

Mexican free-tailed bats **live** in caves.

Mexican free-tailed bats live in huge groups called **colonies**. The biggest colony has almost 20 **million** bats.

11

Olms live in caves.

The olm is a kind of cave **salamander**.
Olms live in caves that are underwater.
They have very light skin and are **blind**.

Cave spiders live in caves.

Young cave spiders sometimes leave the cave. The adults stay in the cave where it is dark. Cave spiders spin webs to catch **insects** and **slugs**.

Cave beetles live in caves.

There are different kinds of cave beetles. Most of them live their whole lives in caves. They cannot survive outside their caves.

Glowworms live in caves.

Glowworms are **insect larvae**. A special kind of glowworm lives in caves in New Zealand. These glowworms are young fungus gnats. They look like hundreds of stars on a cave ceiling.

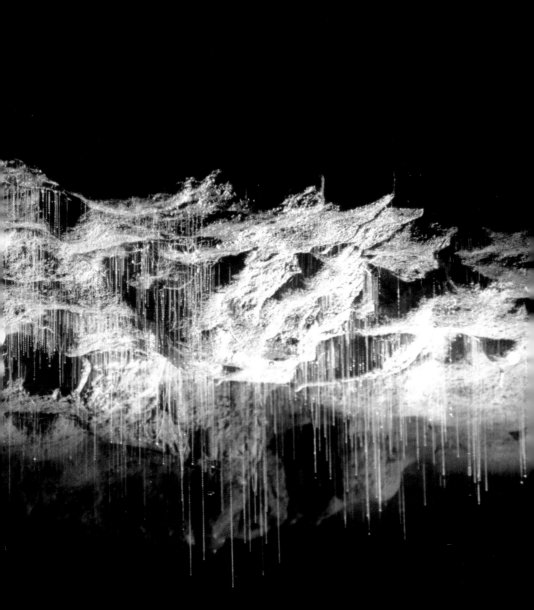

The Somali cavefish lives in a cave.

The Somali cavefish is a **blind** fish. It doesn't need eyes because it's too dark in the cave to see.

Could *you*
live in a cave?